THE CONFIDENT JOB SEEKER

Stand OUT During your Job Search

LAURIE BRADDY

ISBN: 979-8-9886391-0-7 (Ebook)
ISBN: 979-8-9886391-1-4 (paperback)

Interior design by Richell Balansag and Ademir Kalač
Printed in the United States
Published by Laurie Braddy

Dedication

This book is dedicated to my brother Shawn Greaves
who was taken too early by cancer.
I love you so much and miss you every day!

Table of Contents

Introduction

Nobody ever said finding a job was fun. As a matter of fact, it is the antithesis of fun—the thought of resumes, recruiters, and putting on a suit. Being put on the spot to answer, "Why do you believe you are the best fit for this position" (insert dramatic eye roll and air quotes) ad nauseam is enough to make the most socially calibrated individuals twitch uncontrollably.

Here's the thing. We often stay in a job we loathe before treading unknown waters out of fear.

You might not know it, but fear is our primary motivator when making decisions. I could tirelessly quote the psychological research behind this. However, suffice it to say we are more motivated by fear because we have a primal genetic code to search for and avoid danger. This code has shifted from being alert to predators to losing our job or being rejected.

We fear many things when it comes to the job hunt (no ancestral pun intended). Primarily, we fear being unprepared, lacking confidence, or not having the correct answers. We fear looking foolish or being rejected due to a hiccup in our presentation.

But what if you were prepared? What if you had the confidence and answers to refine your resume and hunt down that target dream job with perfect execution?

Whether you are first joining or re-entering the job market, The Confident Job Seeker is the only tool you need. Even if you are a veteran with mid-level experience, you may find that the job-hunting scene has changed. These pages cover that too! From social media tips and answering interview questions, you are bound to gain confidence and find the answers you need to take the fear out of the process.

When the fear is gone—nothing will stop you from standing out and securing the dream job you always wanted! You will get sample questions with answers, see sample resumes and letters, and might even smile at a bit of humor along the way. After all, the job hunt can be an adventure and not the dreary activity of old.

How do I know? Well, I have spent a few years deep in the weeds, so to speak. My name is Laurie Braddy, and I founded the recruiting firm Top Talent Professionals in 2015. I already had fifteen years of recruiting and career coaching experience when I started the business. I moved away from the typical quota system of recruiting firms and focused on a simple approach to job seeking that was fun and results-oriented for my clients. I was on a mission to help them boost their confidence and rock those interviews.

With my placement services, coaching, courses—and this book—I aim to help job seekers navigate the entire process from pre-job search to career advancement. I will take the fear and guesswork out of the process so you can Stand OUT among others in your field!

Chapter 1

Always Stand Out

> *Employers aren't searching for perfection:*
> *they are searching for candidates with*
> *confidence and drive!*
> *~ Laurie Braddy*

Thanks to societal norms and a culture of "compete but fit in," it is no wonder we get mixed signals. We are told to aim for the top—be the best in our class—be a rockstar but don't be arrogant. Then, with the dawn of social media and instant gratification, we feel compelled to use photo filters and carefully curate our lives until they are picture-perfect. We live with the false belief that employers are looking for the "perfect candidate." We answer the call by trying to get noticed or grab attention in unconventional ways.

I will tell you—hold off on the over-the-top TikToks and Instagram reels. Don't feel pressured to define yourself by the latest trend. DO pay attention to your brand. You can be confident without being unnatural.

Brand is a hot topic buzzword these days. When we think of a brand, we think of Nike, the famous swoosh, and "Just Do It." However, we often forget that our personal brand is how we present ourselves to the world and our reputation. So, whether you are actively looking for a new job or think you will at any time in the future—check yourself. Opportunities come at the most unsuspected times, and you never know when you will be unofficially interviewing for your next position.

Personal Branding

Have you ever heard that you should dress for the job you want, not the job you have? The original intent focused on the clothes you wear and how you present your physical person. However, we can argue that in the world of social media, "dressing" can now extend the images, videos, and words you post on platforms. Those platforms are windows to who you are; you are the product in the window. Call it window dressing. Yes, I am sure I have outed my age now. So, if you are not old enough to know what window dressing is, the attractive display in the store window attempts to draw you in when you walk by.

Go to the mall, and you will see window dressing at the front of every store. What they put in the window helps passersby get a glimpse of what the store offers and even a peek at their brand with colors or catchy tag lines. What is displayed in the window helps them stand out against the competition.

Just like these stores, you need to highlight your brand. What are you known for, or what is your reputation? What skills do you have? What interests you? You can exude quiet confidence through personal branding.

We sometimes think our reputation is our brand and will stand alone as social proof. However, your personal brand is something a little different. Reputation is something that is given to you. Your personal brand is curated with intention. Your brand is what you WANT people to see. Harvard Business Review says, "Reputation is about credibility; your personal brand is about visibility and the values you outwardly represent."[1]

Our personal brand will help others decide if they want to be associated with us. So, whether you are in the job market or not, the people who connect with you will often make that decision based on how you present yourself. And today, with how social media works, people are a little more selective in who they connect with.

Don't believe me? Take a look at your Facebook page. Every so often, you will see a carousel of people you "may know" based on contacts. Same with LinkedIn. You will be spoon-fed connection suggestions. Have you ever clicked on those to see who they are or how you know them? What do you see? Have you encountered any that had inappropriate content, so you chose to bypass connecting with that person? Maybe they have nothing but game notifications or political or religious posts that seem to veer past your comfort level.

The point is you are being judged by what you have on these platforms. It is your brand, and if people do not have personal knowledge of your character and who you are, they depend on what they can sleuth from these platforms.

The Social Media Conundrum

Social media gets a bad rap—rightly so in many cases. However, we can use social media for good. Think of it as a tool, like a business card, resume, or the shop window people pass by. You can use social media to create and build your personal brand. It can do the heavy lifting, and you can present a more confident you if done correctly.

Now, if you have some questionable content on your platforms, you might need to do some work. However, once you have the basics, going to each platform and polishing your image isn't too hard. First,

1 Monarth, H. (2022). What's the Point of a Personal Brand?
   https://hbr.org/2022/02/whats-the-point-of-a-personal-brand

you need to think about each platform you are on and the intent of that platform. Think of each as a different social scene.

- **LinkedIn** is a professional networking group. When you hang out here, it is like attending a professional networking event like a conference or seminar. You are there to connect and build professional relationships where you and those you shake hands with can build beneficial relationships for your career, professional, or business advancement. When you build your brand here, it is about your professional accomplishments, skills, and experience.

- **Facebook** is more like a family barbeque. When you hang out here, you will have close family, friends, and even coworkers to chat with. People talk about the weather, family, current events, and of course, the local gossip. Neighbors might pop by to get a recommendation for a good dentist or plumber. Visitors will be everyone from your youngest niece, who got her driver's license to your great grandma, who spends all day playing Candy Crush. She still doesn't know how to turn off the game notifications. When you build your brand here, it is about you as a person and how you interact in your downtime.

- **Instagram** used to be the place for pictures, not words; it was all about the package. Think of Instagram as the local hotspot or nightclub. You will find people of similar ages and interests, but most everyone is focused on showmanship. Carefully curated photos and reels allow users to peacock and vie for attention. The interactions are often more superficial and keeping up with trends and "the vibe" is more important than the depth. This is not to say that Instagram is bad. We all enjoy the clubs at some point. When you hang out here, it is short clips and photos of your highlights—that honeymoon trip to Rome or the guy's fishing weekend. "A picture speaks a thousand words" should be the motto.

- **Twitter** is the place where people feel they can freely interact with celebrities, and everyone has an opinion that is cut to 280 characters or less. You have to be creative and to the point here because it can be a free for all. However, you do have a profile, so make it count. But here's the thing—Twitter doesn't even rank on the charts as one of the most used social platforms. So, if you skip it, it doesn't hurt. As a matter of fact, YouTube is the most used, and Snapchat and TikTok outpace Twitter by a good stretch.

Once you understand the scene, you can modify how you present and build your brand based on the specific platform. You can show some authenticity but confidently stand out. Let's talk about best practices.

Social Media Best Practices

No matter the platform, people will first see a title and photo. With LinkedIn and Facebook, you have your profile photo and a background photo. Be sure to use both! When it comes to photos, consider the following dos and don'ts:

For Photos

 DO—

- Use a current photo of your face (head and shoulders like a headshot).
- Crop the photo properly so your face is clear.

- Keep your expression natural.
- Use background photos that are crisp and clear. If you can't find one, go to Pixabay and download a free one.

❌ PHOTO DON'T—

- Use photos of kids, pets, cars, memes, or random objects (Microsoft eight ball, anyone?)
- Use an outdated photo
- Wear offensive or overly bright clothes, makeup, or hair dye (unless you are an entertainer)
- Use busy or distracting backgrounds
- Use bad-quality photos
- Be overly creative with retouching

For Page Posts and Photos

Consider all of the above for photo and page posts. However, then consider the following:

✔ DO—

- Keep your photos and page posts positive
- Only post if the photo or post will help solve a problem, enlighten, or make someone feel good
- Consider your timing (posting about a celebration on a National Day of Mourning isn't good)
- Post about things you have done, learned, or enjoyed

❌ DON'T—

- Dive into politics, religion, or other polarizing subjects
- Post gossip or things that could be viewed negatively

- Use profanity
- Post cryptic messages

The bottom line is that we often forget who is watching or has access to our social media. Even if you limit who has access, that does not mean someone you know would keep the same discretion. Yes, you can limit who sees what, but a friend of a friend might have enough access to post your "what happens in Vegas stays in Vegas" activities. Moving on!

Let's talk about the other sections of social media and how to capitalize on them so you stand out with confidence.

About Section, Experience, and Bios Oh My!

If you focus most of your attention on LinkedIn, you will be able to carry the information over to other platforms and make small modifications. For this reason, and because this is all about the job seeker, we will mostly address LinkedIn.

The best thing to do here is to open your LinkedIn account on a desktop or laptop so you can get a good view. When you open your account, click on the "view profile" tab and take note of the layout. The first thing you see is the background and profile photo with your name, headline, and area on the left and your current position and education on the right. We covered photos but what about your name and headline?

You want people to recognize the name and face. So, if your name is "Joseph" but everyone calls you "Joe," use Joe. For women, use your legal name, not your maiden name, unless that is how you are addressed. There was a trend on Facebook for women to use their maiden names so classmates from the past could find them and connect. LinkedIn is not that. If you are worried about privacy, you can change how your name shows in the title by going into your settings. You can set your name to show your first name and last initial.

LinkedIn Headlines

Now, let's talk about the headline under your name. It is okay to be a bit creative but don't go over the top or use bad cliches. You want to be searchable by using appropriate keywords, and being overly creative is not rewarded—however, neither is a lack of creativity. For example, telling everyone that you are "Unemployed at Unemployed" is not good (YES, that is out there!). Avoid excessive capitalization, unknown abbreviations, inappropriate language, controversial topics, and emojis and mistakes (grammar, spelling, etc.).

Think about your job title or dream job title. Then emphasize what you do or want to do. However, think of it as a marketing hook. You want to draw attention. LinkedIn will tell you to use your job title and company, but you need to go beyond that. Here are some examples of what NOT to do:

- Don't: Unemployed at Unemployed | (yuck!)
- Don't: Realtor Rockstar at XYZ Real Estate (aren't they all?)
- Don't: Results-driven Accounts Manager at XYZ (cliché)

What you want to do is hit with keywords and grab attention with creativity. You get 120 characters to make a good first impression. Think of it as a one-two-three punch. Think job, then keywords and hook. Consider the following:

- Do: Executive Assistant at Google | Relationship & Leadership Management | A CEO's calendaring problem solver! (105 characters—boom!)

- Do: Executive Assistant at Nike | Relationship & Leadership Management | Quick to solve problems CEOs didn't know they had! (119 characters—boom!)

In these examples, we have the keywords "executive assistant," "leadership management," and "calendaring." You then offer a creative explanation of your skills in solving problems.

From there, you have the About section to expand on and give more details.

LinkedIn About Section

Unlike the headline, the About section gives you 2,600 characters. Similar to the headline, you want to hook the reader and tell a story. Also, be sure to write it in the first person using "I" statements. This makes it feel as if you are talking to the person and a third person is telling them about you. In other words, don't start with "Joe Smith is a top-performing sales team lead. He is respected by his peers and other industry professionals." Be concise, focus on your strengths, and use keywords! Let's go into more detail.

Take the first two or three sentences to convey what sets you apart from others and the number one thing the reader should know about you. You should mention skills, results, or accomplishments and why you do what you do. Take this example:[2]

50% strategist, 50% creative - 100% content marketing specialist. (My Myers-Briggs INTJ-A result doesn't lie!)

The story - your brand's and your client's - is my top priority. My goal is to clarify that story, use it to produce grade-A written and visual content, and

2 Henderson, R. (2023). How to Write a Powerful LinkedIn Summary: Examples and Tips. https://www.jobscan.co/blog/linkedin-summary-examples/#examples_for_professionals_jobseekers

market that content to cultivate the committed audience and conversions of your dreams.

I come to the table with 7 years of marketing experience (in agency, in-house, and freelance consulting settings) and 15 years of experience in the entertainment business.

I wear many hats, but some of my most highly requested offerings include:

- Long-form SEO content (landing pages, blog posts, etc.)
- Short-form content (social media, email marketing)
- Video content production and direction
- Branding strategy
- Development of educational materials (lead magnets, e-books, courses, and workshops)
- Coaching and/or facilitation of public speaking/media relations/presentations.

It is concise and hits on all points right away. The above also uses the keywords that you would see in the industry. When you have the keywords, you will pop up in searches and can be more easily found for your expertise. This person talks about highly requested services and some background. The only thing that could improve this section would be highlighting results and accomplishments. For example, did the service boost a particular company's web ranking? If so, by how much and how long did it take?

Here are two examples that LinkedIn highlights for doing things right:[3]

---

3   Reilly, K. (2022). 14 LinkedIn Profile Summaries That We Love (And How to Boost Your Own). https://www.linkedin.com/business/talent/blog/product-tips/linkedin-profile-summaries-that-we-love-and-how-to-boost-your-own

About

I love selling brands. I hate selling myself. So, here are six quick things about me and my work. In, out, nobody gets hurt.

1.) I've created campaigns for more iconic brands than you can shake an iPhone at. My longtime creative partner, Jag Prabhu, and I have produced work for Unilever. Verizon Wireless. Johnson & Johnson. AT&T. Pfizer. Nestle. Bristol-Myers Squibb, IBM, GlaxoSmithKline. US Airways... And we've gotten to schmooze with the leaders of these fine companies. Quite a rush.

2.) I'm a digital junkie with 23,000 Twitter followers. I love every freakin' thing about the web.

3.) I got my job in advertising in an unusual way. I won a national writing contest called "Write If You Want Work," the brainchild of mega best-selling author James Patterson (Along Came a Spider, Kiss The Girls), then chairman of J. Walter Thompson. My prize? A job as a writer at the agency.

4.) Several years ago, right out of the blue, my funny, active, young(ish) husband was diagnosed with cancer. I mention it here because, ever since, I have liked working on pharmaceutical ads. Some creatives shun them, but not me. Connecting with people over the things that make us human, vulnerable, and imperfect is powerful.

5.) This is how I sum up my job. I help people fall in love with brands. Help agencies win new business. Build trust with clients to help their brands skyrocket. Period. Exclamation point.

6.) I don't like advertising this fact, but I'd do this job for free. It's my passion. Also, aside from advertising, I'm completely unemployable.

Here's the other:

About

One of my first memories in school was going to a parent-teacher conference in kindergarten and having my teacher tell my parents, "Desiree is definitely one of my most talkative; no matter where I move her in class, she communicates with everyone!" Throughout my life, I have developed this art of being able to communicate with anyone at any given time. From joining the debate team in college to studying internal and external communication to working in different careers that allow me to utilize this skill in different ways, I've learned that effective communication is at the core of any successful leader and business.

I have developed a passion for not only being the voice of those that cannot communicate for themselves but also teaching people to communicate effectively. In recruiting, I am able to do this by helping people acknowledge the potential within themselves and be able to communicate that effectively to hiring managers. I am able to communicate with people from all walks of life that all have one thing in common; they NEED A JOB.

Both examples show personality while highlighting experience and accomplishments in a more creative way. When done correctly, you will paint a picture of who you are without having to try so hard in person when opportunities arise. People will have an impression of you, and that will often give you the confidence boost you need to push forward and land that next opportunity.

You can use your profile to exude confidence even if you haven't found it yet. When you have a profile with quality images, it is like putting on a fine-tailored suit and getting a new haircut. You will feel like a million dollars. When you do, the confidence will begin to flow!

Once you have the About section or summary complete, you can move on to experience.

LinkedIn Experience Section

The experience section is laid out like a resume. It is another section that you want to be sure and use keywords and highlight what makes you a rockstar. However, there is a caveat—don't give everything away in the experience section. Share the highlights only! You only have 2,000 characters to make your points. Use active words like "drove," "collaborated," and "negotiated." Avoid using words like "key responsibilities." Also, you can scroll to the very bottom of the profile page and assign skills to your jobs—use it to save space for more impactful words!

Again, this section is about your experience, so focus on what you did and the results as it relates to particular positions or jobs you have had. There is a format that will prompt you, so be sure you fill in all the blanks. You will need the following:

- Your Job Title
- The Type of Employment
- The Company Name (and company logo, if there is one attached)
- The Location of the Company
- The Location Type (onsite, remote, hybrid, etc.)
- Are You in Your Current Role?
- Your Start and End Dates
- The Industry

- Description – This is where you want to highlight achievements.
- Profile Headline – How do you want to be seen? This can be different than the job title.
- Skills – You should have added skills that you can assign to this position. Maybe skills like customer service, Excel, Word, or Photoshop. You can have a list of fifty skills. These are important when it comes to getting recommendations, and they will show in the experience section on your profile.
- Media – Here, you can attach images, videos, and presentations. Be sure to title them because they will show in a headline on your experience profile section.

Another way to use media is to add an introduction video and pin it to the top of your page. To find it, go to the home page of LinkedIn, and where it says, "start a post," you can choose a photo or video, etc., similar to Facebook. Choose a video to upload and ensure it is pinned. Now, there is a caveat. Your video should show the best of you. Be professional and cautious of the video background. We don't want to see dirty clothes, dishes, clutter, or inappropriate material in view. Refrain from including barking dogs and unhappy children— you get the picture.

Finally, you want to spend time on getting recommendations.

Recommendations

Did you know that more than 60 percent of hiring managers will view your LinkedIn profile and other social media? A recommendation is social proof of who you are and what you can do (or say you can do). On LinkedIn, the recommendations section will be at the very bottom of your profile page. You should consider having at least three.

If you don't have any, you should take the time to ask for recommendations. However, when it comes to LinkedIn, sometimes it is better to give before asking to receive. You should go to your recommendations section and open it. Click the "plus" sign, and it will give you a drop-down to choose to either ask for a recommendation or give one. Click on "Give one." Search for a person that you can give a good honest recommendation, and then take your time to write a good one.

When you do this, the other person will be notified that you gave them a recommendation. Wait a few days and then follow up with the person to see if they saw it and if they would like you to revise it. It is at this time that you would ask if they would be gracious enough to reciprocate. Let them know what you are doing and their time is appreciated. If you ask for a recommendation from people you know who are very busy or not good at writing, offer a few sample recommendations for them to use. Let them know you respect their time, and they can copy and paste one if it is easier.

After you have your social media profiles polished, it is time to network.

Social Media Networking

If you haven't done it, consider recording an introduction video and pinning it to the top of your feed. This way, when you are engaging on the platform, others will be able to click on it and get an idea of your personality and what you are doing or looking for.

Now it's time to get active. However, you should be strategic in the days and times you interact with social media. You will want to like and comment on posts when others are active. There are a few studies and several blog posts about the best times to interact on social media platforms. Of course, there are many variables, and they can all change, but the newest data shows the following:[4]

- **HubSpot Says:** Saturdays, Sundays, and Wednesdays between 6 - 9 pm, 3 - 6 pm, or 12 - 3 pm
- **Sprout Social Says:** Tuesdays, Wednesdays, and Thursdays, 10 am to noon,
- **Buffer Says:** Wednesday: 8 am, 9 am, 10 am, 12 pm, 3 pm; Thursday: 9 am, 10 am, 1 pm, 2 pm; Friday: 9 am, 11 am, 12 pm.
- **Oberlo Says:** 10 am to noon on Tuesdays
- **Quintly Says:** Weekdays between 7 am–8 am, at noon, and between 5 pm–6 pm
- **The Balance SMB Says:** Weekdays between 7 am–8 am and 5 pm–6 pm.

The running theme is early mornings, lunchtime, and after business hours.

When you are interacting on social be sure that you are focused on the viewer and what they would want, not you. For example, if someone posts an article or blog, consider asking them a softball question, or if you like the post, give specifics about what you like. The quality of your engagement is more important than scrolling through and clicking the like button on everything.

You will also want to be sure you use the rule we all learned in primary school. If you can't say something nice, don't say anything at all. Your engagement with others should make them feel good and leave them with a positive view of you as a person. You never know who is watching. It could be your future boss. The goal is to draw employers to you, not repel them. Keep your posts in the neutral

---

4   Santora, J. (2023). Best Times to Post on LinkedIn to Increase Your Engagement in 2023

zone—avoid politics, religion, money, vices, etc. Remember, it is not about you but about how you make others feel about you.

Another thing to watch on social media is events. Most organizations and social groups will post upcoming events on social media. They can vary from online events to in-person events and can be recruiting or hiring events to social networking events. Plan to watch for them and then go! If you attend in-person events, treat them as you would a professional event, whether it is or not.

In-Person Networking

There will always be conferences, seminars, recruiting, and social events happening. The key is to interact. However, when interacting, it should be intentional. Let me explain.

An acquaintance of mine said her husband was taking seminars and going to conferences to increase his technical skill and engage with people in the industry. She paid for his travel, and he volunteered at the events to get in for free. The husband had been to four or five events and had been complaining about how unhappy he was with his job. My acquaintance asked him how many decision-makers he talked to at these events. Had he shaken hands and grabbed business cards from other attendees? His blank stare said it all.

She told him that at the next event, he had better bring five business cards home, or she would pay for his travel anymore. As if the clouds had parted and the heavens sang, after the next event, he came home with five business cards and said he was offered a job.

The point is that you must be intentional with how you interact and with who. The above gentleman wasn't a "people person." He was shy and lacked confidence. However, he told his wife that the more he talked to others, the more they wanted to know about him. When other attendees asked him questions, they realized how smart he was and wanted to work with him. He didn't ask them for a job. Other attendees told their bosses they should hire him.

Sometimes it takes talking to others to get a boost of confidence. People will talk to you all day long, but unless you engage with the purpose of finding opportunities, you will go through the motions and travel in circles wondering why you landed at the same place you started. For every person you talk to and hand you shake gets you one person closer to your next boss or coworker. And when that happens, be ready!

Do you have a rockstar resume to give them?

Chapter 2

The Resume of Rock Stars

> *Your resume should represent your expectations, vision, and goals. It's not just about the employer; you matter as well!*
> ~ Laurie Braddy

Recruiters and hiring managers expect them. You do them. However, resumes are the bane of everyone's existence. From the recruiter's and hiring manager's perspective, it is a necessary evil. They ask from them but know what they will get will be riddled with spelling and grammatical errors. If the resume is free from error, then there is always some other thing that gets in the way. Too much fluff and not enough good information is often the problem. However, on occasion, the resume can give everyone a good laugh at the "to err is human" side of job seeking.

So, if we are going to talk about a subject that seems too boring and overdone, consider the following stories shared on JobMob:[5]

---

5   Share, J. (2008). 21 Funny Resume Stories. https://jobmob.co.il/blog/digg-funny-resume-stories/?utm_source=aweber&utm_medium=email&utm_content=9r1a&utm_campaign=blog

"On one of my past resumes, I was lazy and just used a Microsoft Word template. Part of it included an Objective heading and section. I planned to change the objective for each resume I sent out, tailoring it for the job. Anyway, so for the main version, I just entered 'EZ $$$$$$$$$$$$$$$' as the objective, figuring that would be jarring enough for me to change it before printing. The next day I had a total brain failure and sent out about four copies before I remembered 'EZ $$$$$$$$$$$$' was my objective."

OR

"My favorite 'bad resume' was when we were looking for a new Information Security Manager. One guy seemed to have a decent resume, showed he'd even supplied evidence to several federal cases in his time.

He finished by pointing out that he had a book published on the subject of digital forensics and evidence handling ... so we went to Amazon to check it out and found two pages of reviews about how this book was the biggest piece of misinformed, poorly written garbage ever published in the field. We didn't bring him in for an interview.

Moral of the story. Not all published work is stuff you necessarily want to brag about, especially in technical fields; in retrospect, we'd have probably taken him more seriously if we'd found pictures of him downing Jell-o shots."

Yes, resumes can be pure gold when it comes to entertainment. However, unless you are applying for a job as a comedian, it is best to avoid the show. Think rockstar, not comedian.

The problem with resumes is most of us know that automated online tools do the initial vetting. We often wonder how many really look at what is on the page. Resumes are seen as dry, drab strings of information that lack character and are often chock full of exaggerations and the creative use of words. Applicants and job seekers are taught to "fit in," not stand out.

Well, we will fix that.

History and Purpose of the Resume

No, this is not your high school history lesson on resumes. But, you should have a brief overview so you have perspective. First, the word "resume" is French for "resumer," which means "to summarize. It is said that Leanardo Da Vinci was the first to send one when he asked the regent of Milan for a job.

Da Vinci had a letter of introduction, and then he listed his skills and abilities and stated why he believed he was suited for the engineering job. The year was 1482. He didn't get the job, but that doesn't mean that it was the resume. The point is you are in the company of great people when you craft your resume. So, take it seriously and make it shine.

Remember, the purpose of the resume is to open a window. You are trying to give a first impression and help a recruiter or hiring manager determine whether they should weed you out or talk to you in person.

From your perspective, the purpose of the resume needs to address four things:

- What do you want to accomplish with your resume? (New position, career advancement, first job, changing careers, just seeing what's out there)
- What is important to you? (Years in business, company size, mission, technology, culture, training, and development)
- What are your long-term career goals?
- What company(s) do you want to attract?

You want to show that you are not only qualified for the job but that you will fit with the company culture and will support the company goals and mission. You can also give a glimpse of your personality. After all, you need to be memorable but in a good way.

From a recruiter's or hiring manager's view, a job has hundreds of applicants, and a resume is a tool for them to look for the low-hanging fruit and find ways to eliminate applicants. According to LinkedIn, the average time a recruiter will look at a resume on the first glance is six seconds.[6] Read that again. You have six seconds to grab their eye and advance.

You ask, "Seriously, why bother?"

You bother because it is necessary. You need to show you are qualified.

So, how do you make a good first impression in six seconds?

First, today there is no reason for spelling or grammatical errors. We have editing tools in Word and online, and many are free to use. Use them! If you can get past the gauntlet of spelling and grammar mistakes, a recruiter then looks for keywords to see if you are qualified. If they find the keywords they are looking for, they might put your resume in a filtered pile for a second look. This is where words matter.

---

6 Sharma, A. (2019). What Do Recruiters Look For in a Resume at First Glance? https://www.linkedin.com/pulse/what-do-recruiters-look-resume-first-glance-aditya-sharma/

Secret Sauce to Good Resumes

The secret is "there is no secret." There are so many tools for creating resumes that the format and required information are less a question than they used to be. Of course, you can ask 700 people how to structure your resume and get 700 hundred different answers. However, there are a few tips that will help make your resume stand out and above the others. What matters most is being confident and standing out.

First, you have to consider the audience and then consider the words. The first place your resume goes is to the Applicant Tracking System (ATS). These systems are the first to search and filter your resume using keywords. When you focus on the ATS and keywords, it means you will need to adjust your resume to incorporate keywords from the job description. So, every job you apply for might be a different resume. If you get past the ATS, recruiters and hiring managers also look for keywords. So, if you haven't noticed yet—just like a rock band needs a guitarist—your resume needs keywords. Also, your resume will be like a guitar riff where it will be similar in tempo but different to match the audience.

Formatting to Get Noticed

Think of your resume as precious storefront property on Times Square. You don't have a lot of space and need to attract as many prospective employers as possible. With limited space, your resume should not be a detailed account of everything you have done in your professional life. It should be clean, clear, and easy to read, with a synopsis of your skills set, career focus, accomplishments, and end goal. Here are a few tips for using your prime real estate wisely:

- Your resume should go over your history and accomplishments with results. Tell your story in less than 600 words. According to research by TalentWorks that analyzed over 6,000 applicants, the perfect length is between 475-600 words.[7]

- Keep the font simple and use Arial or Times New Roman. Remember, an ATS scans your resume, so the font needs to be ATS-friendly.

- You can avoid the Objective Statement unless you are making a career change or new to the job market.

- Make sure you list your positions in reverse chronological order. Your most current position should be first (at the top) and with the most recent information.

- The resume should be kept to two pages maximum.

- You no longer need to give your full address; the city and state will suffice. However, include your phone number, email address, link to your portfolio site (if you have one), and LinkedIn Profile address!

Now let's talk about experience and education.

Experience, Education, and Gaps

Your experience section should be recent, relevant, and authentic. Do not falsify information. If you don't have the experience, focus on the relevant skills that you have that are transferable. Include accomplishments and results (not just tasks) that are quantifiable. Often it is the human or soft skills that are more important than the hard skills. I can promise you that you have accomplished more than you think. Sometimes, we are our own worst critics. So, take the time to think of your contributions and even consider internships or volunteer work you have done. Finally, remember those pesky

---

7 Sorensen, T. (2020). How Many Words Should
   Your Resume Be? https://www.linkedin.com/pulse/
   how-many-words-should-your-resume-tom-sorensen-headhunter/

keywords. You should be able to sprinkle in keywords from the job description in the experience section.

As for the education section, it should be at the bottom of your resume unless you are a recent graduate. Drop the dates but add any certifications, licenses, awards, and professional development. Also, leave out GPAs unless you are a recent grad with little experience but be sure your GPA was above 3.5.

Now, if you have any gaps in employment, they will be noticed as fast as spinach stuck in your teeth. However, unlike everyone pretending not to see the spinach, you will get called out on gaps in employment. So, own it like you would when the one brave soul points at your teeth. Address it and move on. You should also include the reasons for leaving a position, especially if the position was temporary, the company downsized, or if they closed.

Here are some sample resumes to give you an idea of what yours could look like:

SAMPLE #1
Sample Resume for entry-level candidates

Jill Smith Houston TX
555-555-5555
jillsmith@gmail.com

Career focus (Accounting)

Motivated recent graduate searching for an organization that will appreciate my eagerness to learn and grow.

I want to ease the workload of the accounting department by providing top-notch assistance and doing whatever it takes to accomplish the task at hand. I am a team player experienced in month-end closing and accounts reconciliation. Academic project success in cash flow optimization, inventory management, and accounts receivable. Skilled in reconciling bank statements, credit card reports, and vendor invoices.

Education

Houston University, Bachelor of Science in Accounting 2022
Pursuing my Master's in Accounting & Finance (evening classes)

Accomplishments (Fill this section as much as possible!!!!!)

- Relevant Coursework
- Volunteer work
- Internships
- Professional Development:
- Extracurricular Activities:
- Scholarship Recipient
- Honoree of
- Awarded
- GPA
- Student organization/club member
- Fraternity or sorority member
- Research Project and results of the project
- Dissertation
- Dean's List

Skills

Advanced Excel Spreadsheet Functions

- Audit Tracking

- Sage 50
- Document Management and Storage
- Data Compilation
- PowerPoint Presentations
- AR/AP
- SAP Crystal Reports
- Record Reconciliation
- General Ledger management
- Budget Planning and Analysis
- Data Compilation
- Project Audits
- Accounts Payable/Receivables
- Financial Transactions
- Monthly Closing

SAMPLE #2

Sample Resume for candidates with work experience

John Smith CPA, CFE Ft Lauderdale FL
555-555-5555
johnsmith@gmail.com

Career Focus

Goal-oriented accountant interested in joining a firm that values ongoing training and technology.

Offering 15 years of experience handling finances for individuals and corporations. Diligently maintains the latest training on tax regulations and legal issues impacting financial operations.

Accomplishments

- Introduced and implemented FX ProSystem software which saved my company $750k in overtime payroll.
- Led a team of nine in the development of the "My Accountant" program, which produced $350K in new revenue.
- Developed and executed a client education portal which resulted in an 86% client satisfaction rating.

Professional Experience

ABC Company, Ft Lauderdale FL
Staff Accountant
2015 to Present

Executed financial reporting, managing prepaid accounts, schedules, reconciliations, event settlements, and month end accruals.

Assisted Senior Auditor with year-end financial audits.

Created journal entry schedules to improve efficiency, support, and documentation of accounting processes.

Completed end-of-year financial audits by collaborating with various coworkers.

Increased efficiency, support, and documentation of accounting processes by creating detailed schedules for journal entries.

Analyzed business operations, costs, and revenue in the balance sheet to project future revenue and expenses.

Generated ad hoc reports detailing various metrics and account information.

723 Company, Ft Lauderdale FL
Jr Accountant
2010 to 2015

Interacted with vendors, upper management, and peers.

Managed supplier accounts and built lasting relationships with suppliers.

Submitted weekly cash flow report that showed inflows, outflows, and projections to the controller. Helped clients navigate interactions with tax authorities and legal concerns related to financial matters. Compiled general ledger entries on a short schedule with 700% accuracy.

Maintained integrity of general ledger and chart of accounts. Collected and reported monthly expense variances and explanations

Certifications and Education CPA, CFE, Florida

Florida State University, Bachelor of Science in Accounting, Master of Science- Audit and Financial Accounting

Now that you have an idea of the resume real estate let's talk about where you submit them.

Job Board or Beeline to the Company

Job boards are one of the necessary evils of job seeking. They are convenient for everyone involved. Employers can add job openings, and the job board will run in the background doing much of the heavy lifting. For the job seeker, you can type in a few keywords and generate almost an endless list of job postings based on your keywords. For both sides, job boards are a way to boost visibility and operate 24/7. Because of this ease of use and convenience, everyone does it, and so you are pooled with increased competition for the positions that are posted.

Yes, it is true that you can do searching, and the application process is efficient by clicking a few buttons to submit your resume. Yes, you can more easily track the jobs you have applied for and store all your information in one place. However, the downside is you will also be sorting through tons of redundant and spam listings.

If you are going to post to job boards, which you should, then consider the following advice by Leigh Goessl at the Washington Post:[8]

- Be selective in which job boards you post to. They are not all created equal.
- Be sure you are using keywords and phrases that are relevant but also ones that are related.
- Focus on applying to the newest job posts first. Stale listings should be the last resort.
- Sign up for new listing alerts.
- Add your LinkedIn profile to your information.
- Use other sources beyond job boards, like networking events.

---

8 Goessl, L. (2020). Pros and Cons of Using Job Board to Apply for a Job. https://jobs.washingtonpost.com/article/pros-and-cons-of-using-a-job-board-to-apply-for-a-job/

The biggest thing to remember about job boards, according to Goessl, is "statistics suggest that 80 percent of jobs aren't posted online." When it comes to job hunting, there is an old saying, "It's not what you know, but who you know." So, this means you should be casting a wide net and going beyond your pajamas and job boards. A personal connection can make all the difference. If you see a company post a job on the job board, submit your application, but then go directly to the company.

If you think it doesn't work, think again. I was talking about this with another acquaintance one day, and she was telling me about her son looking for his first job. He was just shy of eighteen and having a hard time trying to get responses. He had applied on job boards and through company websites. She told me that she encouraged him to put on a suit or at least business casual clothes and go to one of the places he applied and ask if the manager was available.

It so happened he had applied to a restaurant chain, and it was close to school and home. So, he took his mom's advice. After school, he got dressed and went to the restaurant. He asked for the manager and explained how he had applied and was eager to have his first job. The story goes that he gave a strong handshake, made eye contact, was polite, and offered his resume. The manager was so impressed the kid was hired on the spot and started the next day.

That was six years ago. Apparently, this young man has used this method throughout his college years for summer jobs and has been hired on the spot every year. Yes, he has his resume. However, he is also a walking rock star resume. That first experience built his confidence, and now he doesn't rely on job boards. Job boards are a tool and the first step in the process of standing out.

When you have a rock star resume and can master the technology, and understand that it is only a tool, you will be miles ahead of the competition. The cream rises to the top, and that is when you get the interview!

Interview Like a Pop Star

Is the interview a dreaded activity for you, or do you see it as your time to shine? If you are like most, the interview phase can be as about as fun as a dentist appointment (no offense to my dentist). However, if you think of it as your opportunity to be on stage, in the spotlight, and belting out your favorite tune in perfect harmony while the crowd roars with admiration, would that change your mind?

I can hear you now. I can't sing. I seriously dislike being in the spotlight. Nobody in their right mind likes being on stage in a crowd of strangers.

I get it. We can't all be Taylor Swift. But, we can learn to be a legend in our own minds (in a healthy way). You must remember that if you have made it to the interview, you have successfully beaten the ATS. You have captured the attention of the recruiter or hiring manager within six seconds. You rose to the top and stood out more than all other potential candidates. So, you are already a pop star.

Have confidence that the decision-maker already sees you as part of an elite group.

If you approach the interview with this knowledge, it will help you relax and focus on what matters. From there, it is about preparation. The interview phase is broken into three parts, the pre-interview, the interview, and the post-interview. Each one plays a critical role. Let's start with the pre-interview.

Pre Interview Phase

The Roman philosopher Seneca said, "Luck is what happens when preparation meets opportunity." The opportunity is the interview, so prepare for it like you are a teenage boy planning his first date. Not sure what I mean?

First, you can be so excited that you got the "yes" for a date that you forget to get the other person's contact information. Don't do that. Be sure you have the interviewer's contact information. If it will be a video interview, get the link or address and directions if you are meeting in person.

Then, you want to know as much as possible about the company. Sleuth the company website, their social media, and any recent news about the company. Take notes about the company's mission statement, their goals, and anything they value through recent accomplishments. You should be able to explain the company's product or service. Then, research the person or people who will interview you. What are their interests and industry presence? This could be the one thing that sets you apart. For example, I knew a tech guy who tinkered with classic cars. It was not well-known. However, a young man was getting ready to interview, and this guy was the first on the list of three interviews. The young man worked classic cars into the interview, and the two hit it off. The interviewer said he didn't really remember much about the other candidates.

Once you have all this information, figure out how you integrate it with their mission and goals. What skills or beliefs do you have that would help to achieve their future plans? How would you fit into the company culture?

From there, you need to prepare for the interview. Will it be in person, a call, or a video? Each one will need different preparation.

If you plan to meet in person, you need to know how long it will take you to get to the location. Consider driving to that location a few days before the interview to see if any unexpected delays like road construction could occur. Figure out where you will need to park and how long it might take to get to the office location from where you park. Finally, consider the time of day you will go. Could there be additional traffic delays?

You will also want to be sure that you dress the part. There is something to be said for dressing for the job you want and not the one you have. Several studies have shown that how we dress affects our cognition, sense of worth, and confidence.[9] One study demonstrated that wearing formal clothes improves negotiating and persuasion skills.[10]

Consider dark and neutral colors and traditional business attire unless the job is more creative or clearly gives you instructions about dress codes. Avoid oversized jewelry, heavy perfumes and makeup, and clothes that are dirty, wrinkled, ill-fitting, or could be offensive. Finally, be sure to pay close attention to hygiene. I know it might sound crazy to say it but brush your teeth and hair. If you feel the need

---

9 Slepian, M. L., Ferber, S. N., Gold, J. M., & Rutchick, A. M. (2015). The Cognitive Consequences of Formal Clothing. Social Psychological and Personality Science, 6(6), 661–668. https://doi.org/10.1177/1948550615579462

10 Kraus, M. W., & Mendes, W. B. (2014). Sartorial symbols of social class elicit class-consistent behavioral and physiological responses: A dyadic approach. Journal of Experimental Psychology: General, 143(6), 2330–2340. https://doi.org/10.1037/xge0000023

to wear something bright or flashy, consider one piece of statement jewelry or colorful socks with your suit. Plan your wardrobe early!

If your interview is by phone or video, ensure you have the proper equipment and check to see if it works. Test it more than once. You might find that you need to update software or applications. Do this the day before the interview so you can avoid technical difficulties. Plan to have the call or video in a quiet room so that the background is void of distractions and clean. The last thing you want is your unmentionables showing up in a Zoom video. If you are on video, dress as if you are in person. Remember, what you wear could impact your cognition, confidence, and power of persuasion!

The next thing to consider when preparing is practicing how to answer questions that could be asked and preparing some questions of your own. There is nothing worse than being caught off guard by questions or freezing when asked if you have any questions. So, first, let's run through possible questions that could be asked of you.

Consider how you would answer the following:

- Tell me about yourself.
- What are your greatest strengths?
- What are your biggest weaknesses?
- Why do you want to work for this company?
- What do you know about our company?
- What relevant experience do you have?
- How do you handle stress or pressure?
- How do you prioritize your work?
- What are your long-term career goals?
- What motivates you in your job?
- How do you handle conflicts with colleagues or supervisors?
- Can you provide an example of a time when you went above and beyond for a customer/client?
- How do you stay up to date on industry developments and trends?

- What type of work environment do you thrive in?
- Can you provide an example of a challenging project you completed and how you overcame the obstacles?
- What type of management style do you prefer?
- How do you handle constructive criticism or feedback?
- Can you provide an example of a time when you had to work with a difficult coworker?
- How do you handle tight deadlines?
- What questions do you have for us?

It's important to note that different companies and industries may ask different questions, but the questions above are quite common in many types of interviews.

Conversely, be prepared to ask some questions of your own. Consider asking the following:

- What are the key responsibilities of this position?
- What is the company culture like?
- What do you think are the biggest challenges facing the company right now?
- How do you measure success in this role?
- Can you provide more details about the team I would be working with?
- What opportunities for growth and advancement are there within the company?
- How does the company support professional development and training?
- What is the typical career path for someone in this role?
- How does the company support work-life balance?
- Can you tell me more about the position goals?
- What qualities do successful employees at the company have in common?
- How does the company approach diversity and inclusion?

- Can you walk me through a typical day or week in this role?
- Can you tell me about a recent successful project the team has worked on?
- How does the company stay current and innovate in its industry?
- What do you enjoy most about working for this company?
- How long has this position been vacant, and why?
- How has this vacancy affected your company/department?

Power Questions to ask toward the end of the interview:

- Thinking back to a previous employee who excelled in this role, what made them stand out?
- What tasks/projects need to be executed immediately?
- What is your timeline for making your decision, and when can I expect to hear back?
- What additional information do you need from me to make a decision?

These questions can help you get a better sense of the company and the role and demonstrate your interest and engagement during the interview.

Speaking of—

The In-Person Interview

When the interview day arrives, the first thing to remember is to be yourself. Interview anxiety is natural. However, if you study your questions and prepare, you will rock your interview. Embrace quiet confidence. As you prepare ready yourself, remember a few tips for the day:

Show up early and be ready to impress. You should time how long it takes to drive to your destination if you meet in person. Also, account for any walking if you must park some distance from the meeting place. Consider whether you need time to check in or find a specific location within a building. When you arrive early, you give yourself time to calm down and catch your breath.

Mind your manners. This sounds easy enough. However, we often forget some of the subtle habits we have. Refrain from answers that are anything other than clear "yes" or "no." For example, avoid head nods or the "yeah" and "nah" responses.

Other tips include the following:

- Make sure the job description, prepared questions, and accomplishments/challenges are in front of you.
- Let the interviewer take the lead!
- DON'T overtalk the interviewer(s)!
- DON'T exaggerate anything, be prepared to explain the process of XYZ.
- If you are asked a question to which you don't know the answer, tell the truth and explain that you will research, learn, and become educated.

Tips for Phone and Video Interviews

If you have a phone or video interview, follow all of the above but keep the following in mind:

Phone Interview

- In my opinion, this is the toughest method (no visuals to build trust, no body language, etc.)
- Pick a quiet place!
- Speak clearly and speak up!

Video Interview

- Test your internet connection or WIFI BEFORE joining the meeting.
- Sign on 5-15 minutes early.
- Dress to impress!
- Prepare for the unexpected (power outage, internet issues).
- Ensure your background is clean and professional.

No matter which type of interview you participate in, be sure to end on a positive note. You want to be memorable. If you are genuinely interested in the position, end with one of the following:

- I really enjoyed meeting with you/your team, and I am 100 percent interested in joining your company.
- My interest level is very high because................ (make this about them)
- Is there anything I can demonstrate further that would catapult me to the top of the candidate list?
- I am so excited to get started!

Then leave yourself an opening to follow up post-interview.

Post Interview

The post-interview can be a time to shine like that rockstar on stage. Many people fail to follow through, but those who do often get rewarded. First, send a thank you note. Send a thank you note to the interviewers within twenty-four hours of the interview! Make sure to include critical points—why you want the position, the value or impact you will add, and how you match their culture and skill set.

Did you know that if two candidates are a match—one sends a thank you note, the other does not —nine times out of ten, the interviewer will choose the candidate that sent the thank you note? It shows follow-up, motivation, determination, and etiquette.

Here is a sample thank you note for reference:

Subject line: Thank you for meeting with me

Greetings Madonna,

Thank you for taking the time to meet with me yesterday afternoon. I enjoyed our conversation and learning more about the Accounting Manager position and the team at ABC company!

I was very impressed with you and your company! This appears to be a rewarding role, especially given the opportunities for collaboration and advancement. My master's in accounting and prior experience within a public accounting firm would work well in this role.

I look forward to possibly joining your team. Please do not hesitate to contact me if you need additional information about my background.

Thank you, Michael Jackson
Mike.jackson@email.com
723-456-7897

Then you wait for the offer or no offer.

Offer/No Offer, Now What?

If you received an offer, congratulations! Here is what you need to do before accepting:

- The initial offer usually would first be a phone call. Thank them for the offer.
- Get the offer in writing. You want to go over the offer.
- Review the entire offer. Make sure it includes salary, benefits, vacation, position, start date, and probationary period.
- Review the objectives in the offer. Are they realistic? When do you need to decide to accept? Generally, you need to accept or decline within forty-eight hours.
- Negotiate the offer. Is the salary what you asked for?
- Benefits? Vacation?
- Give yourself some time to make sure this is the right opportunity. Take twenty-four hours to digest the offer.
- Accepting: Do you need to give notice to your current employer?
- Giving Notice. Give notice in person, over the phone, and in writing. Do not burn bridges.
- Declining the Offer: Declining an offer should be done over the phone and a follow-up email thanking them for the offer and reasons for not accepting (if you want to
- tell them).

But what happens if you don't get an offer?

Didn't Get the Offer?

You have a choice of three reactions here.

- Express anger and hostility, go on the defense, and spend the next two weeks trying to discover why you weren't chosen.

- Go away quietly.
- Act like a professional, and THANK them for considering you.

You still want to leave a GREAT impression! The company WILL remember how professional you were, and you may end up receiving a call back for another position!

Here is what you can do to stand out.

- Send a thank you note! Thank the organization for the opportunity!
- Connect with the hiring managers on LinkedIn (wait at least a couple of weeks to do this)
- Follow the Organization on LinkedIn

Sample no offer thank you note:

Hello Mr. Man,

Although I wasn't chosen for the Accounting Manager position, I want to thank you and your team for considering me. I really enjoyed meeting everyone and would welcome another opportunity to interview with ABC company in the future.

Sincerely, Donald Duck

No matter what you do, be honest, be confident, and be YOURSELF!

From here, it is time to get back in the game.

Chapter 4

Get Back in the Game Post Layoff or Termination

As a society, we are judged and assessed by our occupation. Therefore, when we are laid off or terminated, it can have monumental effects on our psyche. With the initial shock, you may go through bouts of anger, asking Why me? and worrying about how you will pay the bills. Losing a job comes with the same stress level and emotions as losing a loved one, moving, or planning a big wedding or event. All of these are life changing BUT temporary. You will get through it! While you process the situation and get through the initial shock, there are some things you should and shouldn't do.

✖ DON'T:

- Make it a mission to get back at your former employer or manager. This is a waste of time.
- Listen or engage in gossip with employees currently working with your former employer.
- Sit around too long; get back up!
- Listen to negative people!
- Listen to 700 people telling you what you should do.
- Rush out and take a crap job out of desperation.

✔ DO:

- Spend some time alone and ignore everyone for a bit. You need this.
- File for unemployment benefits if you are eligible. This step can be very stressful, but you need to get this out of the way first.
- Surround yourself with successful people if you can.
- Get your resume, social media accounts, networking skills, interviewing skills, and POSITIVE attitude ready to take on the world!
- Write yourself a forgiveness statement/letter. This might sound stupid, BUT you need to do this. If unfamiliar, a forgiveness statement/letter is a letter you write to yourself to let go of anything weighing you down. It is about finding inner peace and not being so hard on yourself.
- Finally, update your resume!

Prepare to Re-Enter the Job Market

This period of initial shock and cycle of emotions may ebb and flow. It is crucial to take this time off, focus on immediate needs, and reset your mindset. Of course, if you file for unemployment, you can bridge the gap in income for a while. However, you may need to consider savings and other means to take care of your immediate needs while you prepare to re-enter the job market.

Getting laid off or terminated can give the ego a knock-out blow. Therefore, time is of the essence to focus on your strengths. You will want to revisit the resume section to update your resume. Think about recent accomplishments that need to be added. From there, update your social media profiles, and consider who is friends and foe in your network. Who will you reach out to? Consider volunteering or taking a certification or class. This can help explain your gap in employment!

Finally, prepare to answer for the elephant in the room. Inevitably, an interviewer will ask for an explanation when they see the gap. Don't let this scare you, almost everyone has some sort of gap and being prepared to "fill in the blanks" is all you need to do. We are all human and things happen.

Prepare an Explanation

Terminations are either justified or frivolous—only you and your previous employer know the truth. Inquire whether your former employer will give you a reference (this is important). Even though you were terminated, they may still be inclined to give you one. Check the laws of your state; some employers can NOT give negative information. If you held that position for shorter than a year, leave it off your resume.

Learn from the termination (no one is perfect). You want to be able to answer for the gap or termination but also offer a positive outcome. Consider what important lesson you learned or knowledge you gained through the experience.

It is often natural that some of the anger from a termination will carry over into your first interview. We tend to be defensive after a termination and want to shift the blame to anyone but ourselves. DON'T show resentment for your former employer in the interview; this happens all the time. Remember to be positive.

What does your termination explanation look like? Write this while calm and then memorize it.

Chapter 5

Stand Out for
Raises and Promotions

Believing you are worthy of a raise or a promotion is one thing. Convincing someone or a group of people that you deserve it can be another story. Employees are often denied a raise or promotion because they are unsure how to justify the reasoning for either. First, most employees will lump raises and promotions together. However, they are very different animals.

Raises and promotions are completely different and require different approaches. A raise means you are requesting more money or better benefits for doing the same job. A promotion means you are asking for more responsibilities, a management role perhaps, or any role within the company that is above your current level. More money usually accompanies a promotion but not always.

Before asking for either, you should be able to articulate the reasons why you deserve it. For example, perhaps your responsibilities have increased, or you have been loyal and haven't received a pay increase for a while. Think about your recent accomplishments. Have you saved the company money? Are you efficient or willingly take on more work when asked? Have you completed a special project or solved a problem? Maybe you have trained or mentored new employees or finished a training program?

Write down all you do and have done in the last twelve months.

The Raise

If asking for a raise, consider the following tips to prepare for the ask:

- You should now have solid reasons why you feel you deserve a raise; now, you need to justify them.
- DON'T expect your current employer to know everything you've accomplished; chances are they don't realize what you've done.
- "I work really hard" is NOT a reason to ask for a raise! We should all be working hard! You need to produce clear, detailed, and quantifiable proof of your success within the company.
- Get your resume ready! Yes, you read that correctly! This will show your employer that you are serious.
- Your resume needs to include your current employer! Tasks, accomplishments, awards, projects, kudos, the little extras, etc.)
- Research the marketplace for salary information on your job title and be armed with the information.
- What do you want? You need to know this BEFORE the meeting! Salary, bonus, PTO, etc.

The Promotion

If you are asking for a promotion, consider the following tips to prepare:

- Asking for a promotion is a lot different than asking for a raise. It's not just about how much more money you want–it's about how much more responsibility and accountability you're willing to take on.
- Will you be leading a team? Taking on special projects? Developing new policies/procedures? Maybe you are already taking on responsibilities that are above your current job title, and you want an official promotion.
- You need to update your resume and treat this process as if you are interviewing for a new position (because you are).
- Determining exactly what position/department you're striving for is important. Once you understand the expectations of the position/department and EXACTLY what's involved, write up a mini business plan or plan of action explaining how your career goals align with the company's needs and why it makes sense for them to give you more responsibilities.
- What changes do you want to see within your compensation package? Be specific and write it down.

Consider writing a mini business or action plan. The plan should include what you will do in the first ninety days after the promotion. If ninety days is too soon for your goals, pick another timeframe. Your plan should include a current problem and YOUR solution. If no problems exist (rare), then go with an "I want to be part of making our wonderful company even better" route.

Business or Action Plan

Here are a couple of example plans.

Example #1:

We have a lot of clients who want to work with us, but we lack the resources to connect with them at the level they expect and deserve.

Within the first ninety days, I will implement a new client system that allows us to interact with our clients more effectively.

This new system will accomplish this goal by providing better support for our customers as well as making it easier for them to use our services.

It also allows us to cut down on expenses by automating some processes that were previously done manually.

Example #2:

The accounting department is currently facing high turnover, which is costing our company time and money.

In my first 90 days, I will determine the reason for this and develop an employee program that will result in a happier workforce which will save time and money by retaining the talent we already have.

I also plan to implement additional training programs that focus on soft skills such as communication, teamwork, problem-solving, etc.

These types of programs are important because they help employees feel more confident about themselves and their ability to perform well at work, which can make them feel more satisfied with their jobs overall - leading to less turnover!

WRITE YOUR ACTION PLAN.

Once you have your action plan written, ask your manager for the time to meet. You want to schedule this meeting so that your employer or boss is prepared to speak with you and allows adequate time for the conversation. This is not a topic to approach passing in the hall. Tell your employer you would like to discuss your future with the company and what you have to offer.

If you are asking for a raise, consider this script:

> "I have been with our company for four years now and have learned so much in that time. I am grateful for the opportunity to work here, and I am excited to be a part of this organization's future growth and success.
>
> I want to bring to your attention some of the successes I've had since my last salary review (or since I started with this company). Here is my current resume, which also includes several accomplishments, awards, and special projects.
>
> I currently make XYZ with an X% bonus; I would like to increase that to ABC with a Y% bonus."

If you are asking for a promotion, relax and exude confidence. You are fully prepared for this meeting and ready to deliver your presentation (yes, it's a presentation).

Treat this meeting like you are interviewing for a new position (which you are). Then consider saying something like:

> "I believe that I have proven my value to the company and have demonstrated my abilities to complete tasks above and beyond my job description.

I am requesting that my compensation package reflect my value to this company.

I have prepared an action plan to support my vision and eagerness to help our company achieve great success."

When you approach asking for a raise or promotion by doing these things, you will have much better success. However, a raise or promotion is never guaranteed.

What to Do if You Are Turned Down

Being turned down for a raise or promotion is hard to swallow but try to stay positive (for the moment). You need to ask for specifics why you were denied (this is critical).

Maybe you are not ready or deserving of a raise or promotion, but chances are you do deserve that raise or promotion since you have invested time and money to be prepared. If you are truly worthy, consider shifting the conversation and asking what you could do to get the raise or promotion. See if you and the decision maker can map out a plan for what you want and how to get it.

If shifting to the conversation doesn't work and there doesn't look to be hope for a raise or promotion in the future, you must decide whether to stay with your company or start searching for a new opportunity. If you have truly been a star employee and have demonstrated your worth to the company, it may be time to make a change.

No matter your industry or job title, there are employers out there that WILL see your worth and compensate you accordingly and/or place you in a position that is better suited for growth.

The key is to wait until you are calm and clear-headed before making a decision. If you decide to start looking for other opportunities, get your resume ready and put all the relevant information you gathered for the raise and promotion meeting to add to your resume.

Whether you get the promotion, raise, or find a new opportunity, it will be essential to shine in your first 90 days.

Chapter 6

Hit a Homerun in Your First 90 Days of Employment

Your first 90 days of employment are highly crucial and will set the tone for your future! Don't be afraid to make your mark, make yourself unforgettable, and make a lasting impression that will follow you for the rest of your career.
~ Laurie Braddy

The first ninety days of employment sets the tone for your future within the company. You want to capture attention immediately, avoid toxic coworkers, discuss your monthly performance, and assess your value and progress at the ninety-day mark.

Capture Attention

From the beginning, you should know what the expectations are. If you don't, ask. Ask your boss this question on DAY ONE: Thinking about the most successful person you've had in this role, what made them so successful? (if you didnt ask during the interview).

All eyes are on you when you first start with a new company. Keep your radar on high speed and watch what is going on all around you. Take the initiative by:

- Being willing to learn and ask tons of questions.
- Take on tasks that nobody wants.
- When a problem arises or when someone needs help, offer a solution, or offer to help (if you can assist).
- Ask for additional responsibilities if possible.
- If you are required to attend meetings, speak up during these meetings.
- Outwork everyone in your department!
- From there, showcase your capabilities by:
- Using your experience, and don't be afraid to complete tasks or projects your way (they hired you for your experience).
- If you have deadlines to meet, beat them!
- Critical thinking is key.
- Master your time management skills.
- If you are in a client-facing or end-user role, go the extra mile with each client (word will get around).
- Keep track of key accomplishments (this is important for later). You want to track accomplishments so you can bring them up at your ninety-day review.

If you do all of the above, you should be too busy to fall into the gossip trap of toxic coworkers.

Avoid Toxic Coworkers

While this may seem like an irrelevant topic, I believe it's a very important topic that needs to be discussed. I have seen numerous employees destroy their career goals (sometimes their careers) all because they fell into this foolish trap.

We all want to fit in with our peers whenever we start with a new company. Regardless of company size, you WILL have people waiting in line to give you the scoop on everyone and everything. While some information may be truthful, most will be pure gossip from employees who are not happy, usually due to their own performance issues or lack of drive and motivation.

Don't fall into the "misery loves company" trap! This is a surefire way to destroy your positive momentum and keep you from achieving your goals.

Remember, if these people are so unhappy, why are they still working there? Ignore them; you will eventually figure out the landscape on your own.

Be prepared for these people ahead of time. You will encounter them your entire career! Every time you engage with a toxic coworker, you are inviting them to disrupt YOUR career goals! This is your time to stand out in a productive and positive way! So, how will you stay positive, stay on track to reach your goals, and fend off these people? Have a plan.

Finally, stand out by discussing monthly performance.

Monthly Performance Tracking

Most companies will give you a performance review after ninety days of employment or at least a detailed discussion regarding your performance. However, you can stand out by initiating a performance discussion with your boss each month. No one does this, even though it has proven valuable repeatedly. For those that attempt the exercise, they use it looking for a pat on the back. Don't do this!

Have your performance tracker with you for each of these meetings. When you go into your meeting, exude confidence and give examples. For example:

- I introduced an easier way to connect with our clients during the XYZ project; please tell me your thoughts.
- I gave a lot of thought to our current ABC problem, and I have some ideas. Would you like to hear them?
- My department is having a few end-user issues with the new software; I believe I can make this rollout hurt a little less; here is my solution . . .
- Could you please share with me the company's sales goals for Q2? I want to be a part of the company's success!

Then consider asking some questions like:

- How is my performance thus far? Does it measure up to expectations?
- Are there any areas that need improvement?
- If you are in a non-structured training, ask your boss if you could move to the next phase of training (assuming you are ready).
- If you are in structured training, ask your boss if you could speed it up (assuming you are ready).

If you track your monthly progress, you will be better prepared for your ninety-day review.

The Ninety-Day Performance Evaluation

The first thing you want to do before your ninety-day review is to determine your value. Have you made an impact? Do you have a roadmap of your performance and accomplishments? Did you rectify issues or improve where needed? Then think about what you expect or want to happen.

Here is a sample ninety-day review:

Sample Ninety-Day Performance Evaluation (employer)

| Employee Name: |
| Position: |
| Supervisor: |
| Department: |
| Date: |

Period of Work under Consideration:

1. What areas of the employee's work performance are meeting job performance standards?

2. In what areas is improvement needed during the next six to twelve months?

3. What factors or events that are beyond the employee's control may affect (positively or negatively) their ability to accomplish planned results during the next six to twelve months?

4. What specific strengths has the employee demonstrated on this job that should be more fully used during the next six to twelve months?

5. List two or three areas (if applicable) in which the employee needs to improve their performance during the next six to twelve months (gaps in knowledge or experience, skill development needs, behavior modifications that affect job performance, etc.)

6. Based on your consideration of items 1–5 above, summarize your mutual objectives:

   A. What the supervisor will do:
   B. What employee will do:
   C. Date for next progress check or to reevaluate objectives:
   D. Data/evidence that will be used to observe and/or measure progress:

Supervisor Signature: _____________________ Date: __________

Employee Signature: _____________________ Date: __________

Once you make it past your ninety-day review, it is important to maintain your resume, social profiles, and performance tracking. The one constant in life is change, and you should always be ready!

There is a saying that you never know when you are talking to your next boss. In the final chapter, explore how and when you should make changes to profiles and resumes and consider new opportunities.

Chapter 7

Always Stand Out and Be Employable

Once employed, we tend to get comfortable, and the pain and headaches of job hunting disappear. It is only in the time of panic when we are faced with a layoff or frustration over a missed raise or promotion, that we feel the need to dust off the resume and start shaking hands again.

I know it sounds about as fun as a root canal, but updating your resume, keeping current social profiles, and working to broaden your network are much easier to manage if you maintain it during downtimes. Consider ongoing maintenance if you are in an industry with high turnover or mobility (like technology). Do the following:

- Annually or bi-annually, update your resume with recent training, accomplishments, and awards.
- Once a year, update your professional photo for social media and profiles. The first of the year is a good time. New beginnings and all!

- Engage with contacts on LinkedIn and your professional networks at least quarterly.

Also, think about maintaining your ongoing image.

Maintain Your Image

The comfort of coworkers and positions will sneak up on you. It is natural to let your guard down and become more casual in certain situations. However, never lose sight of the fact that you should maintain a professional image in your work and career. Too often, a bad Christmas party stint can impact your career trajectory. Consider practicing the following:

- Always dress appropriately. No matter what industry, dress a half step above everyone else.
- Watch your language. Refrain from getting too comfortable with slang, cursing, or lazy language like "dude" and "bro." Elevate your language a step above everyone else.
- Volunteer your time. This doesn't mean doing free work or taking on the work of less motivated coworkers. However, find ways in which you can support a noble cause. If you see the janitor struggling with opening a door while carrying something, open and hold the door.
- Stay positive. Smiles are contagious, but so is negativity. Choose the path that could brighten someone's day. Be part of a solution and not the problem.

If you do the above, you will be in a better position to ask for referrals, raises, promotions, and new opportunities. Coworkers, supervisors, and new employers will be drawn to you because you stand out as a prime example of the most employable.

From there, stay in the know and seek out knowledge or experience.

Lifelong Learning

No matter what industry you are in, there will be changes. Changes in technology touch every aspect of life. Systems and processes are upgraded and improved. Even how we communicate seems to change.

You will not stay relevant if you do not embrace learning and knowledge. This does not mean that you have to go back to school and get an advanced degree. However, you should consider staying up to date with what is happening in your industry and beyond. Consider the following:

- Subscribe to industry publications and read articles related to your position or company.
- Take a seminar, listen to a podcast, or go to a conference relevant to your industry.
- Join a club or professional organization.

It doesn't take much to stay ahead of everyone else. Having the knowledge that others do not helps you stand out when it counts. Even learning how current trends and the economy impact your business or industry can give you a leading edge.

Finally, having a recruiter and career coach in your corner is always good. Yes, this is a shameless plug to connect! Please feel free to check us out https://toptalentprofessionals.com/ www.careercoachingnow.com

Thank you for reading The Confident Job Seeker! I wish you much success now and in the future, you got this!!!!!